LAST DA
OF THE
OLD CORRIS

GWYN BRIWNANT JONES

GOMER

ABBREVIATIONS USED IN THE TEXT

CRS Corris Railway Society
DTM District Traffic Manager
LCGB Locomotive Club of Great Britain
LGRP Locomotive and General Railway Photographs
M&GoW Museum and Galleries of Wales
NRM National Railway Museum, York
NM&GoW National Museums and Galleries of Wales

AUTHOR'S NOTE FOR 2003 EDITION

Events since publication of *The Last Days of the Old Corris* in 2001 have rendered obsolete part of the text on page 5. The 'crowning achievement to date', for example, is now undoubtedly the carriage of fare-paying passengers from Corris – initially on 3 June 2002 – for the first time in 72 years. Official celebrations and grand opening are planned for 7 June 2003.

The subsequent extension of the line southwards towards Pont Ifans and Tan-y-coed now becomes an increasingly realistic proposition. The story of the Corris continues . . .

Caption to title page picture.
Ticket window and Booking Office door at Corris station, photographed during May 1965 by G. H. Platt.
Courtesy W. G. Rear

Contents

Acknowledgements

Grateful thanks are extended to Roger Carpenter, Richard Casserley, Alan Jarvis, John Keylock, and Roger Kidner for assistance with prints, either from their own collections or featuring the work of R. K. Cope or H. C. Casserley.

Similarly, Richard Greenhough and the Corris Railway Society have been most supportive, as also have Dr Dyfed Elis-Gruffydd and staff at Gomer Press, Llandysul.

Gwyn Briwnant Jones
Cardiff, 2001

First impression—2001
Second impression—2003

ISBN 1 85902 011 9

Printed in Wales at
Gomer Press, Llandysul, Ceredigion

PREFACE

WHEN *Great Western Corris* was published in 1994 a sequel, concentrating on the line's final days, was virtually unimaginable. All relevant material then available had been incorporated in the earlier title but, since publication, further information and photographs have come to light. A new impression of *Great Western Corris* (due for publication Autumn 2001) was initially thought to provide an opportunity to incorporate some of this material in an appendix but such was the quantity discovered that this slim souvenir now emerges in its own right.

An 1831 map of the Liberty of Machynlleth, for example, surveyed expressly for that year's Parliamentary Reform Bill, has helped to throw interesting new light on the meanderings of the river Dyfi, the official cause of the line's demise. This suggests that the events of 1948 were not entirely unpredictable to anyone with basic knowledge of the river's past behaviour; such developments could have been forestalled by the railway authorities well in advance of events, had they so chosen.

More importantly, however, is the resurgence of part of the old line under the aegis of the increasingly effective Corris Railway Society (CRS) founded in 1966. Despite the passage of over half a century since closure, it seems that interest in the Corris is undiminished. The early years of the CRS were undoubtedly difficult times but the tenacity of the pioneering members has triumphed; with resilience, energy and perseverance, they have once more established Maes-poeth as the engineering headquarters of a 2ft-3ins gauge railway which wends its way between slate fences *en route* to Corris. The society is now in the process of bringing this track

up to passenger-carrying standard and building, initially, a basic terminus at Corris, alongside the well-established museum in the old company's stable block.

New rolling stock is being constructed and examples of some of the unique waggons which once operated on the line are being restored or replicated. The crowning achievement, to date, is the successful launch of a project to build a near replica of one of the line's last steam engines, the Kerr Stuart built 0-4-2T, No. 4. Further funds (some £20,000) are still required to complete this project but with over twice that amount already raised and put to good use, construction of the locomotive is well-advanced at the Daventry premises of Winson Engineering.

Restoration of the whole route, however desirable, is not possible, but after achieving the restoration of passenger services between Corris and Maes-poeth—hopefully in the not too distant future—this ambitious society entertains high hopes of then extending southwards to Esgairgeiliog and as far as the Forestry Commission's picnic site at Tan-y-coed.

Throughout the volume, 'up' journeys are those when travelling up-valley from Machynlleth to Aberllefenni, in the best traditions of the old Corris Railway, unlike the GWR practice, when Machynlleth-Aberllefenni trains were regarded as 'down' services.

The *Last Days of the Old Corris* is basically a picture album, incorporating views which may not have received too much exposure in the past. The final pages by Richard Greenhough, on behalf of the Corris Society, form a logical link between the past and the emerging railway.

An Introduction to the Photographs and Photographers

The Photographs

THE format of *Last Days of the Old Corris* has been influenced by the number and nature of the photographs which have emerged since publication of *Great Western Corris*. These are presented in two main groups: the first, representing the railway during its later years of operation; the second, portraying the period immediately following closure.

The images used in Part I, under the heading The Last Years of Operation, draw on the work of a number of photographers who visited the line, including Stanhope Baker, Lewis Cozens, Selwyn Pearce Higgins, Roger Kidner, Arthur E. Rimmer and P. Ransome Wallis, whilst the official GW photographer recorded withdrawn rolling-stock – two views of Corris timber waggons on the scrap pile at Swindon are included here. Part I concludes with a brief log of a journey along the line by Arthur E. Rimmer in 1939.

In Part II, After the Closure, plates 31–53, with three exceptions, feature the work of H. C. and R. M. Casserley. All their photographs herein were taken on Monday, 23 August 1948, the first day of closure of the old Corris Railway. Together with the contribution of R. K. Cope, who visited the railway a month later and again the following year, they form an invaluable record of a period in the history of the Corris which is easily overlooked. Initially, perhaps, these photographs were considered to have only a limited, rather morbid appeal, but they have been gradually re-evaluated over the years and, viewed collectively, the Casserley and Cope prints served as the inspiration for this modest souvenir.

Whilst the quality of the majority of the photographs is of a high order, some tolerance is required regarding a few prints which have been included because of their unusual content. The first two images are examples in this category as both are derived from severe enlargements of portions of commercial postcards. The originals portray Machynlleth as seen from the hill behind Penrhyn Dyfi and these fragments, although imperfect, are included as they provide tantalising glimpses of the railway stations during the opening decades of the twentieth century. One or two other prints which are technically weak will hopefully prove to be sufficiently interesting to justify their inclusion.

The Photographers

1. STANHOPE W. BAKER

Stanhope W. Baker first photographed railways in central Wales, including the Corris, in 1932; he returned in 1947, 1948 and 1956. Although he regarded himself as 'being mean with film' and his Corris pictures as only 'fairly average' he nonetheless produced some charming work and is thought to be the only photographer who recorded transhipment of slates and slabs on the Aberllefenni wharf at Machynlleth. In July 1948, less than a month before closure of the line, he had to decline the offer of a trip on the train to Aberllefenni as the driver 'could not guarantee what time he would be back and I had a [main line] train to catch . . .'

2. H. C. and R. M. CASSERLEY

Few who have planned a railway visit can have experienced the disappointment which awaited H. C. and R. M. Casserley as they stepped from the 1.10 p.m. 'down' train at Machynlleth on Monday, 23 August 1948. Armed with official passes for a journey from Machynlleth Low Level to Aberllefenni, they were looking forward to at last adding the Corris Railway to their unique collection of British railway photographs, but matters did not go according to plan. Richard Casserley has no clear recollection of precisely who imparted the sad news of the demise of the little line but, presented with such disappointing news, it would have been understandable had they left without taking any photographs at all, or at most, just one or two of the sheeted Nos. 3 and 4 on their lonely siding. But thankfully, as Richard recently recalled, his father 'had an itchy trigger-finger' and in addition to the obligatory engine portraits and one or two general views of the Low Level station site, both walked the line to the damaged river embankment and beyond, through Ffridd Woods. Despite being *sans* steam the resultant photographs are a unique record of the Corris 'on the morning after'. They not only record the hours immediately following the cancellation but, quite incidentally, portray the line just as it had appeared on countless mornings during the previous decade, when the little train made its way up the Dulas valley with coal and general merchandise, and returned later in the day with slates, slabs . . . and moss!

The steel rails, as ever, were ready to accept the train on the morning of 23 August, had the river not intervened. No. 3 had been prepared, the boiler was full and the bunker coaled; it only required a fire to raise some steam—wheels and motion were oiled and ready to turn. Despite the protective canvas drawn across the cab, the Casserley photographs portray well the state of readiness of the little Falcon that morning.

3. R. K. COPE

R. K. Cope is known to have photographed the Corris on at least two occasions; on the first, he arrived a month or so after the last train but the atmosphere of the Corris must have appealed to him for he returned on a second occasion,

approximately a year later to record some of the final scenes of decay. As he was able to venture as far as Aberllefenni, his photographs complement those of H. C. and R. M. Casserley who were confined to the lower reaches of the line. It is much regretted that neither Cope nor Casserley were able to record the line in operation.

4. LEWIS COZENS

Lewis Cozens appeared not to be particularly interested in photography but is included here as he revealed a great affection for the smaller lines of mid Wales during the immediate post-Second World War years. Whilst others, notably W. E. Hayward and Selwyn Pearce Higgins, had visited the Corris and recorded aspects of its development and decline, Cozens was the first to attempt a history of the line. Various historic accounts have appeared over the years, but Cozens' work, based whenever possible on research from primary sources, still has much to commend it.

5. W. J. K. DAVIES

The W. J. K. Davies photographs were taken not by the well-known author of narrow-gauge topics but by a youthful William John Keith Davies, known to his contemporaries in Machynlleth as Ardwyn. Sadly, he died when still a young man but, fortunately, a few contact prints of his work survive. The exposures and prints were made in 1948 but the negatives (including, incidentally, one of a GW 28xx at Barmouth Junction) are long lost.

6. SELWYN PEARCE HIGGINS

Selwyn Pearce Higgins was another who was charmed by the Corris during its years of decline. He had been introduced to the railways of the area during holidays at Borth, from the mid 1920s but, as he regretted, did not discover the Corris until the 1940s. He then paid the line several visits and even managed to take a few photographs during the difficult war years.

7. IFOR HIGGON

Ifor Higgon of Arthog noted and photographed the Cambrian lines avidly between 1924 and 1967 but, for some reason, virtually ignored the Corris Railway. The four photographs he took of the Corris engines were all taken at Machynlleth. He appears not to have visited other parts of the line and it is much regretted that he seems to have been unaware of the worn-out remnants of Nos. 1 and 3 which lay in the Upper Corris branch siding at Maes-poeth during the 1920s.

8. ROGER KIDNER

Roger Kidner, the prolific author and publisher, has also admired the Corris for a great number of years. Although he has been attracted by the narrow-gauge rails along the Dulas valley it might be pertinent to say that he has been equally drawn by the quarries and the quarry lines themselves. From a photographic point of view, it appears he was unlucky with weather and light conditions when he photographed the Corris *per se* but better weather seems to have accompanied him whenever he took to the quarries.

9. G. H. PLATT

Geoffrey Platt is not thought to have photographed the Corris until 1965, when he recorded the view of the Booking Office window – one of the tangible remains of the old line at that time which subsequently disappeared.

10. ARTHUR E. RIMMER

The Rimmer photographs have been loaned by John Keylock. Arthur Rimmer is known to have paid the line a visit in 1939, on an occasion bless'd with glorious sunshine. Two of the resulting photographs appear in *Narrow Gauge Railways in Mid-Wales* (J. I. C. Boyd, 1970) and a third, undated but with the identical train formation, appeared in *The Railway Magazine* for June 1941, p. 270. The photographs here reproduced may, possibly, pre-date the 'sunny' visit and because of the poor light encountered on this occasion, may have served to inspire a second visit; but this is pure supposition. It is apparent, however, that these images pre-date the wartime scrap drive of 1940.

11. P. RANSOME WALLIS

It proved an unexpected pleasure, whilst searching through the photographic files at the National Railway Museum, York, to discover that P. Ransome Wallis had paid the Corris a visit in 1939 but, given his standing amongst the first rank of railway photographers, it was somewhat disappointing to discover that only three engine portraits had resulted (one each of Nos 3 and 4, and one of the pair together). Only the portrait of Driver Humphreys and No. 4, the 'duty' engine on the day of his visit, is included.

12. F. A. WYCHERLEY

The only Corris image by this photographer was discovered a matter of days before the front cover of the book was finalised; it provides us with a striking portrait of engine No. 4 and Driver Humphreys.

Part I
THE LAST YEARS OF OPERATION

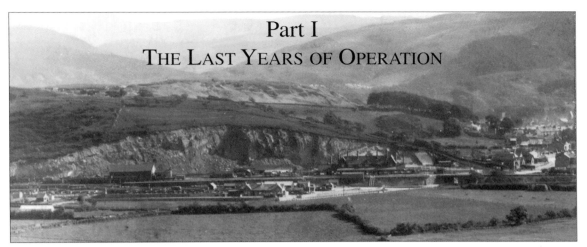

1. Though this image is understandably lacking in definition, it is nevertheless possible to discern, from left to right, a narrow-gauge weigh-house; a stable (with window and door); signal-box (with sloping roof); six waggons of slates/slabs waiting on the grade up to the Braich-goch wharf; the long wall along which the carriage shed was later built; the new station building with short carriage/bus shelter alongside; one carriage and brake-van in front of the station building; recently constructed entrance and wall; an indication of the location of the curved siding to the Abercwmeiddew wharf and, finally, the double flight of steep steps to the Cambrian station. Possible date of photograph *c*.1907/08.   *GBJ Coll.*

2. This later view, although a dark print, allows us to make out (from left to right) part of the corrugated iron carriage shed and a locomotive running around two carriages. A further two carriages and van are parked at the end of the sidings. At least two buses add to the air of congestion, as does a lorry/horse-dray parked across the end of the siding. The rear of the station sign (seen on p. 12) can be made out and the curve of the Abercwmeiddew siding is again represented, but the flight of steps to the high level has been removed and replaced by the sloping path below the mainline waiting-room. A 'down' GW passenger train is hauled by what appears to be a 'Duke' class engine whilst the main road, near the Corris station entrance and beneath the main line bridge, appears wet—perhaps the aftermath of a Dyfi valley flood? *c.* 1925.   *GBJ Coll.*

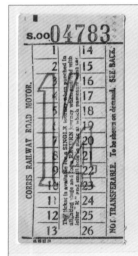

CAMBRIAN AND CORRIS R^LYS

TICKETS ISSUED HERE

— FOR —

RAIL AND COACH

EXCURSIONS

3. This photocopied image is of a badly damaged example of a type of enamel sign displayed outside selected shops in the area which served as agents for the sale of tickets, including combined road-rail tours to Tal-y-llyn.
Courtesy M. Lloyd

4. Corris Railway Road Motor tickets.
Trefor David Collection
Courtesy Mrs Ann David

5. Brass-rubbing of a catch-plate from a Corris Railway Guard's cash bag.
GBJ Coll.

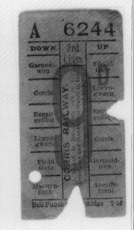

10

6. Corris Railway tickets.

Trefor David Collection
Courtesy Mrs Ann David

7. Photographs which feature the large wooden 'sight-screen' at the end of the line at Machynlleth are not numerous. The screen is just discernible between the end of the last coach and the adjacent van. No. 4 waits with the 7.00 p.m. train which was timed to connect with the evening mail train from Aberystwyth and the coast. 5 April 1926.

LCGB Kenn Nunn Coll.

8. This image, copied from a small contact print, is currently the only known photograph showing the front of the sign which advertised the Corris Railway to main line passengers at the Cambrian's Machynlleth station. Although partly obscured by the private waggon and the stock of coal on Lumley's wharf, the board may be seen to have been some 6-7 ft wide and between 3 and 4 ft deep, which could have provided useful space for the display of posters and other notices. *c.* 1928.

Mike Lloyd Coll.

9. Contrasts at Swindon. The newly refurbished main line rolling-stock at the head of this photograph, and protected by a red flag over the coupling of the *Mica*, contrasts with the scrap in the foreground. The carcasses of at least eight Corris Railway timber waggons can be made out as well as, somewhat unusually, what appears to be a solitary flat car. Photograph dated 6 November 1930.

M&GoW

10. It might seem at first glance that this close-up was taken on the same occasion as the above photograph but, rather surprisingly, it is dated 13 December 1930.

M&GoW

11. Kerr, Stuart & Co. Ltd., No. 4047, Corris Railway No. 4, waited at Machynlleth with an Aberllefenni train during the last months of independent passenger service; 24 May 1930.   *Ifor Higgon*

12. Having crossed the Dyfi, No. 4 attacked the 1 in 32 gradient up to Ffridd Gate on a miserably wet occasion in March 1939.   *Roger Kidner*

13. This view of No. 3 by Stanhope W. Baker was taken on the same date as the wider view featured on the dust-wrapper of *Great Western Corris*; both have their virtues. No. 3 lost its vacuum pipe sometime during the 1930s but it was still evident at this time, as was the large box (of sand?) in front of the smoke-box door. Photograph dated 29 June 1932.

S. W. Baker

14. No. 4 was the engine in steam when P. Ransome Wallis visited Maes-poeth in 1939; the precise date is not known, but a youthful Driver Humphreys was obviously persuaded to draw No. 3 from the depth of the shed for another photograph. The short siding in the foreground, although strewn with ash and clinker, shows signs of periodic use.

P. Ransome Wallis

15. The first of five (undated) contact prints by Arthur E. Rimmer, kindly loaned by John Keylock. Prevailing weather conditions, the limitations of pre-war film and commercial processing have all contributed to extremely heavy shadows which virtually obliterate all locomotive detail, but fortunately this is well-recorded by other photographers. These prints are notable for their atmospheric qualities; they capture well the dismal conditions of a wet summer's day.

The siding at Llwyn-gwern, commendably free of long grass, may just be noticed in the distance between van and station building. *c.*1939.

Arthur E. Rimmer

16. No. 3 with its single waggon of coal and van negotiates the sharp curve between Llwyn-gwern and Tan-y-coed, *c.*1939.

Arthur E. Rimmer

17. North of Tan-y-coed; this stretch of line will hopefully be restored and see steam again. *c.*1939.

Arthur E. Rimmer

18. Taking water at Maes-poeth from the tank located within the shed roof, a ploy to avoid freezing-up during winter months. *c.*1939.

Arthur E. Rimmer

19. Price Owen appears ready to continue towards Corris. The presence in the photograph of the signal-box and signal-post in the middle distance are further indications that this series of photographs was taken before the scrap drive of 1940.   *Arthur E. Rimmer*

20. No. 3's slumber was disturbed on another occasion, for the benefit of Selwyn Pearce Higgins, when this attractive portrait resulted. Waggon No. 31997 was possibly in for some minor repair but, more likely, had contained loco coal and was due to be returned to Machynlleth. Photograph undated, but possibly 8 January 1943. *NRM/Selwyn Pearce Higgins*

21. At Llwyn-gwern station, Price Owen has left his van and is about to open the crossing gates. The waggon of lime, immediately behind No. 4, was destined for Matthews Mill siding, otherwise the only freight on this 'up' journey appears to be in the van; it cannot have left much room for the guard and Selwyn Pearce Higgins, who travelled that day. All the quarry waggons carried owner's plates, whilst the three slab waggons, interestingly, appear to have trestles of different heights. Photograph dated 8 January 1943.

NRM/Selwyn Pearce Higgins

22. An attractive view of the train, set in the time-worn but still much used station at Corris. The youngsters, complete with pet dog and home-made pram (a typical example of wartime make-do-and-mend) provide a delightful cameo of village life. In contrast, the train is largely ignored, apparently taken for granted. GWR cart No. 1275 rests on the coal wharf. Photograph dated 8 January 1943.

NRM/Selwyn Pearce Higgins

23. No. 3 at home; whether at the beginning or the end of the day is not apparent but if the exhaust resulted from use of the 'blower', rather than the photographer's use of a slow shutter speed, then this exposure was probably made during the morning's steam-raising session. The long pit was partly filled-in during the 1930s—possibly to reduce maintenance and also as it was no longer essential. The machinery in Maes-poeth was very basic at this time. Photograph dated 5 September 1947. *NRM/Selwyn Pearce Higgins*

24. An atmospheric view taken from the point where the former siding serving the Ratgoed wharf at Machynlleth (partly visible on the right, but here used as a GPO telegraph-pole store) crossed the connecting line to the Aberllefenni wharf, behind the camera. This section has been liberally treated with weed-killer, in an attempt to eliminate wheel-slip, although the gradient does not appear difficult from this angle.

The remains of an early morning haze above the Dyfi floodplain augers well for a fine spring day. Photograph undated but possibly 19 April 1948.   *NRM/LGRP*

25. The morning light favoured the photographer as he composed this attractive record of the girder bridge across the Dyfi. The low water reveals the neglected state of the concrete foundations of the piers—particularly that nearest the camera—where the flow of the river was usually most intense. The bridge itself, however, seems sound enough to last out the century, and more. Photograph dated 19 April 1948.   *NRM/LGRP*

THE branch here was built initially for traffic from the ERA and Cambrian Wynne quarries and slate works (opposite). The bridge across the Dulas at this point proved equally convenient for villagers who used the trains and later became the subject of dispute when it was allowed to fall into disrepair. Mr Dix, the Corris manager at the time, solved the passengers' side of the problem by selling some second-hand timber to the villagers, allowing them to construct their own footbridge across the river. An agreement was later reached between the railway and quarry companies, that if the Corris assisted with the repair, it would have free use of the bridge 'as and when required'. Slate traffic then continued but slowly dwindled during the 1920s, diminishing to 25 tons by rail in 1925, nil in 1926 and a further (and possibly final) 3 tons in 1927. Information supplied to H. Warwick, District Traffic Manager (DTM) Oswestry, on 13 October 1930 states: '. . . no traffic is carried over the bridge at present, nor for the past 2 years as the tramroad and the bridge itself is [sic] considered unsafe'.

This source also indicates that the small amount of coal traffic for Esgairgeiliog was taken on to Corris for delivery by horse and cart at this time, causing the DTM to query the rate of 5s. 6d. per ton (carriage & delivery) for coal traffic to Esgairgeiliog, as opposed to 4s. 9d. to Corris. When the bridge was in order, the rate was 4s. 9d. per ton (carriage & delivery) although no actual delivery was made by the company as nearly all houses were situated close to the tramroad and the coal was collected by the consignees; often, the empty waggons were returned by them to the head of the siding although, occasionally, a horse from

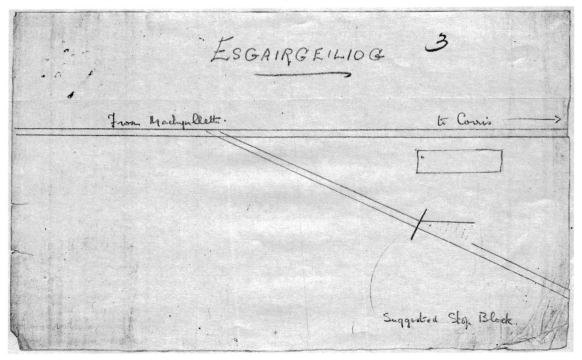

Corris had to be sent down to tow the waggons nearer the main line.

Stop-blocks were erected around the time of the above correspondence (December 1930/January 1931) at both Llwyn-gwern and Esgairgeiliog sidings, the former at the point from which the rails to Llwyn-gwern quarry were taken up and, at Esgairgeiliog, as illustrated and indicated on the sketch—probably drawn by T. Griffiths, former PW ganger, Corris Co. Removal of one rail from the section beyond the block was obviously not considered essential, for all the track below the block survived *in situ* for a further eighteen years or so, until finally lifted *c.*1948. The rails on the main line side of the block formed a siding which saw periodic use until *c.*1940.

26. This undated photograph appears to be one of a series taken during the spring of 1948; it reflects the need at that time for additional rails to replace worn or broken examples elsewhere on the system. This short section was obviously seen as a further source of steel rail; the phenomenon of broken rails is not a new development.

The huts on the brow of the hill were known locally as The Camp. They were constructed initially by/for the unemployed during the 1930s but eventually served several purposes until demolition finally freed the site for more permanent housing in the 1950s. During the war period they housed a borstal-type institution known as the Norton Training School; on Monday morning, 31 August 1942, three of the inmates absconded and reached Machynlleth undetected but were later spotted by an eagle-eyed porter in an empty waggon on a goods train (*County Times* 5 Sept 1942). Photographed, possibly, on 19 April 1948.   *NRM/LGRP*

27. No. 3, with Robert Price Owen and Driver Humphreys (the latter apparently camera conscious on this occasion) set their train back to pick up the guard's van before departing for Aberllefenni on 22 March 1948. *W. J. K. Davies*

28. When Station Master Cambell Thomas and H. Briwnant Jones accompanied Lewis Cozens on his visit to the line on Wednesday, 9 June 1948, only a solitary waggon separated engine and van on the 'up' journey that day. Guard Price Owen was persuaded to pose alongside the train but Driver Humphreys, although just visible, remains discreetly within the cab. No visible reminders of the passenger loop remain at this date and the site of the former inspection pit (extreme left) is overtaken by the notorious Japanese knotweed. *Lewis Cozens*

29. After arrival alongside the former passenger platform at Aberllefenni, the guard walked back to hold the points for the train to be reversed into the loop. This allowed the engine to run around its train and extract it through the points at the southern end before propelling it past the camera position, onto the quarry system. This slightly more time-consuming manoeuvre was necessary during the final years as the inspection pit, located in the loop-line, was declared unsafe to bear the weight of the locomotive. 9 July 1948.

GBJ

30. This decidedly poor photographic image is only included here as it portrays the very last train on the old Corris Railway. The final 'down' service was met between Abergarfan and Doldderwen by two cyclists who had set out from Machynlleth to enjoy, once more, the sight of the *trên bach* in the Dulas valley. It was not then realised that this was the final journey. Driver Humphreys, friendly as always, obligingly brought the train to a halt for the camera but the photographer, using a rare and very slow Dufay 127 colour film for the first time, lacked sufficient experience to realise that the fixed exposure of his simple camera could not cope with the dense shadows caused by the heavy foliage behind the train. Despite a blue sky and sunshine, the severely under-exposed transparency which resulted was a great disappointment. In an effort to obtain an improved image Wallace Heaton of New Bond Street was commissioned to attempt a black and white copy. The transparency has long since disappeared; only the black and white copy, which has remained in the shadows in every sense, now survives. 20 August 1948.

GBJ

A Journey on the Corris Railway in 1939

THE following notes by Arthur E. Rimmer (courtesy John Keylock) may be unique; they are believed to be the only log of a journey on the Corris to emerge to date. Despite the omission of explanatory notes and other details, they form a fascinating account, and because of their rather sketchy nature they are reproduced as seen. A copy of the relevant page of the GW service timetable for the summer of 1938 is printed beneath, for comparison.

It seems that Rimmer intended the jottings solely for his own use and was not to know that twenty-first-century enthusiasts, whilst delighting in his photographs, would analyse his timings and, far from being content with them, would seek to furnish some of the missing information by reading 'between the lines'.

A few timing enigmas, such as '1.35–1.45 Esgairgeiliog' and the allowance of just 3 minutes for taking water at Maes-poeth, become more fascinating on close scrutiny. Foremost amongst the omissions lies the fact that some of the times quoted fail to indicate whether they record arrival or departure. Equally importantly, there is no explanation for the fact that both legs of the journey ran decidedly late. In the 'up' direction, arrival at Aberllefenni was 15 minutes late (disregarding the 5 minute late departure from Machynlleth). Furthermore, 27 minutes were taken between (supposed) arrival at Llwyn-gwern and arrival at Maes-poeth, a distance of precisely 2 miles. In independent days, 25 minutes proved sufficient for mixed and passenger trains to cover the whole distance between Machynlleth and Corris (5 m.) and during the GW regime, 25 minutes were adequate for light engine movements between Maes-poeth and Machynlleth (4 m. 22ch.).

Regrettably, although the date is noted, no reference is made to weather conditions. Was this trip, perhaps, undertaken on a fine day when, possibly, the crew had stopped 'in section' to point out some particular aspect of the view or the railway's earlier history; or was this the occasion of the 'wet' visit, when Rimmer's journey might have been plagued by a greasy rail? No mention is made of such possibilities although a note alongside the Maes-poeth time suggests an urgent need for water, but the bracketed word is not entirely legible. Had there been problems with a greasy rail in this section, both the time and the water situation could have been affected. Arthur E. Rimmer might be surprised to learn that such possibilities could exercise the minds of Corris enthusiasts over six decades after his visit, yet it would add considerably to our interest and satisfaction had more details been recorded. The lack of information about the load on the 'up' journey may be attributable to a light, 'unexciting' load, because the 12 full waggons on the return trip were certainly noteworthy, as is the fact that the timing indicates that these were treated with great respect on the 'down' run, which occupied a full hour and a half; 32 minutes over schedule. The great care required with such a heavy train could be a further indication of difficult rail conditions *en route*, but it is not conclusive.

At present, therefore, we have no way of knowing if the notes are related to any of Rimmer's photographs.

CORRIS RAILWAY [Tuesday], 27 June 1939

12.45 from Corris
Hasty meal loaded cakes & candles.

No. 3 0-4-2T shunting. Falcon Engine & Car Works Loughborough.

1.05 dep. [for] Ffridd Gate . . . crossing gates. Steep climb from here, curving.*

1.25 Llwyngwern . . . open gates.

1.35–1.45 Esgairgeiliog.

1.48 Evans Bridge Crossing.

1.52 Maespoeth [urgent?] water.   No. 4 Kerr Stuart 0-4-2T.
Old signals   Good track
Stopped water till 1.55

2.00 Corris, dep. 2.05   Carriage sheds empty; covered station.

2.14 Garneddwen Crossing gates.

2.20 arr. Aberllefenni
Shunting and getting full 12 wagons slate slabs.

2.45 dep. Aberllefenni.

3.10 Corris

3.17–3.22 Maespoeth

3.35 Esgairgeiliog

3.50 Llwyngwern

4.10 Fridd Gate

4.17 Machynlleth.
Shunting   Driver Humphries [sic], Guard Price [Owen]

*The 'steep climb' surely refers to the 1 in 32 gradient from the Dyfi bridge, which was encountered before Ffridd Gate (although the curves commenced here).

CORRIS BRANCH.

(NARROW GAUGE.)   (Worked by one engine in steam.)   **Week Days only.**

Miles from Machynlleth		DOWN TRAINS. STATIONS.	K Goods SO	K Goods SX	G L.E. SX	UP TRAINS. STATIONS.	G Goods SO	K Goods MO	K Goods SO	G L.E. MSX	K Goods SX
M.	C.		a.m.	p.m.	p.m.		a.m.	noon.	noon.	p.m.	p.m.
—	—	MACHYNLLETH ..dep.	10 45	1 0	4‖5	ABERLLEFENI . dep.	..	—	12 0	—	2 30
—	38	Ffridd Gate .... ,,	—	—	—	Matthews Mill S. ,,	....	—	CR	—	CR
2	22	Llwyngwern Sdg. ,,	ST	ST	—	Garneddwen.... ,,	....	—	CR	—	CR
3	44	Esgairgeliog Sdg. ,,	ST	ST	—	Corris .... { arr. { dep.	....	—	CR	—	CR
4	22	Maespoeth.....	—	—	4‖30	Maespoeth...... ,,	10‖0	12 0	12 30	12‖15	CR
5	0	Corris .... { arr. { dep.	CR	CR	..	Esgairgeliog Sdg. ,,	—	CR	—	—	CR
5	65	Garneddwen.... ,,	—	—	..	Llwyngwern Sdg. ,,	—	CR	—	—	CR
6	8	Matthews Mill S. ,,	ST	ST	..	Ffridd Gate .... ,,	—	—	....	—	CR
6	41	ABERLLEFENI . arr.	11 45	2 0	....	MACHYNLLETH arr.	10‖25	12 40	....	12‖40	3 30

Part II

AFTER THE CLOSURE

The Casserley photographs were all taken on Monday, 23 August 1948.

31. A broadside view of No. 3 on that fateful morning. Driver Humphreys had done what he could to protect the little engine, not only by securing canvas over the cab but by applying a liberal dose of oil to the motion and by placing a piece of slate over the chimney to prevent water entering and corroding the smoke-box. The number-plate, still on the locomotive that morning, was removed shortly afterwards by the fitters at Machynlleth.   *R. M. Casserley*

32. A fine portrait of No. 3 in 'ready-to-run' condition.   *H. C. Casserley*

28

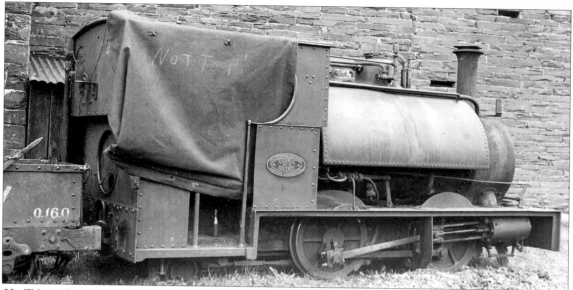

33. This particularly evocative view of the little Falcon that morning, records clearly the slightly enigmatic message 'NOT TO BE' chalked on the canvas (see *Great Western Corris*, p. 66). A further reason for this cryptic message is suggested by study of this print; could it just have been a case of not enough chalk? After the motion had been oiled, the empty bottle was left on the footplate.   *H. C. Casserley*

34. An end-on view of the coal transfer siding behind the station building at Machynlleth. The decidedly irregular bridge rails on the left of the picture, running down from the erstwhile Braich-goch wharf, were little used after the mid 1920s and not at all during the 1940s, despite the fitting of a new lockable wheel-stop on the gradient c.1942. The steel rail siding which served as Nos. 3 and 4's final resting place on the Corris originally formed the through route to the Abercwmeiddew siding, across the standard-gauge yard.   *H. C. Casserley*

35. Steel and wooden-bodied waggons stand on the coal transfer siding at Machynlleth, waiting for loads which will never materialise on the Corris; sheeted No. 4 and condemned waggon No. 31987 lie alongside. *H. C. Casserley*

36. Steel dram No. 32000 and a variety of standard-gauge trucks present an interesting comparison between the two gauges. *H. C. Casserley*

37. Solitary dram No. 31992 stands on the goods loop-line virtually on the site of the former narrow-gauge weigh-table, which was removed during the scrap drive *c*.1940.

H. C. Casserley

38. A youthful Richard Casserley waits on board the brake van for the journey that never took place. That the van had been unlocked could suggest that R. P. Owen had started to follow his normal morning routine before he received the news that the train was not to run, but the *Liverpool Daily Post* reported that the railway was 'officially closed on August 22, 1948' – the previous day.

H. C. Casserley

39. Thereafter, the van remained locked for several weeks before it was hand-shunted alongside the old coaling stage, nearer the locomotives. It was transferred to Tywyn on 7 April 1951.   *H. C. Casserley*

40. This was the general view that greeted those who sought to travel by rail to Corris during the 1930s and '40s. The isolated van would indicate that the engine either had not arrived from Maes-poeth or that it had not yet completed its shunting.   *H. C. Casserley*

41. The reverse view. The short bus garage, used by coal merchant Huw Lumley's delivery lorry during the 1940s, is visible in the distance, at an angle to the main station building. The site of the larger carriage/bus shed, demolished *c*.1939/40, is indicated by the high-level wall and concrete pit remains (l/h). The former passenger run-around loop lay to the right of the long siding holding the van. What appears to be a standard-gauge van near the station building was, in reality, the grounded GW *Iron Mink* which served as a coal store.   *H. C. Casserley*

42. The approach to Machynlleth from the north, showing the start of the goods loop and the inclined access to the Aberllefenni transfer wharf, location of some ferocious slipping when the rails were greasy. The small shed on the wharf, centre of the picture, served as an office-cum-shelter for Mr William Breese who normally transhipped the slabs and slates. The Low Level station building is visible, extreme right.   *H. C. Casserley*

THE CULVERT

43. The culvert, just north of the location of the previous photograph, again looking towards Machynlleth.

H. C. Casserley.

A map prepared by Lieut. Robert Dawson R.E., for the Parliamentary Reform Bill of 1831, contains some of the earliest professionally surveyed evidence of the restless nature of the river Dyfi. It reveals a bifurcation of the river near Craig-y-bwch which created two courses between that point and immediately east of Dyfi bridge, where both channels united.

Gradually, over the ensuing century, the Dyfi settled for the more northern of these two routes and, eventually, both entry and exit points of the southern course became silted, leaving only a short isolated section between 50 and 100 yards long (depending on the season). This lay directly across the route of the Corris Railway and had to be crossed by laying rails and sleepers across two massive baulks of timber, keyed into the foundation stonework. The depth of water here could vary between about 12 inches, during a dry season (yes, there used to be dry seasons) and

about 36-40 inches or so when the river was high, or 5–6ft or more, when in flood.

Sight of the culvert was a key factor in deciding whether enginemen would venture their train through any flood water. If the culvert was flooded, the service was suspended.

During the 1930s and '40s, it became apparent that the river was again becoming restless. The GWR engineers were forced to erect groynes at several points in the river west of Cemmes Road, including Craig-y-bwch, to protect the main line. These proved successful but as the 1940s progressed it was obvious that the river was still truculent and anxious to claim its former course west of Craig-y-bwch. Its rebellion started in earnest at the point where it had previously digressed, but the engineer was ready and forced it back towards its prime course through several groynes and revetments (which may still be seen, now isolated in the meadow). The work in the immediate area was successful but once it was well clear of the main line the river's progress was unfettered and there was nothing to prevent it from destroying acres of tender alluvial meadow, down-river, with each succeeding flood. Not only was the river allowed to continue this destruction, the railway authorities now seemed to look upon its petulance with favour; no groynes were erected to protect the Corris.

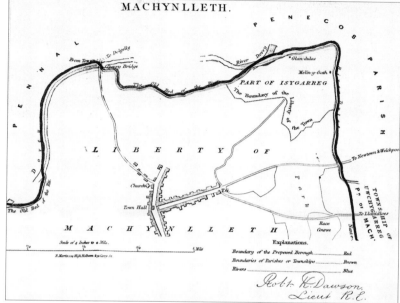

44. Parliamentary Reform Bill Survey Map, 1831.
Courtesy H. G. Wilson

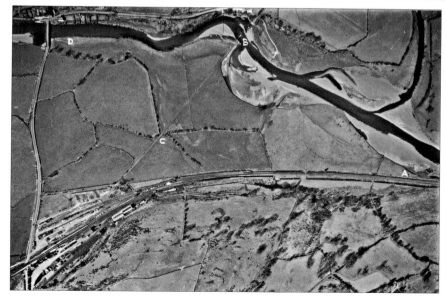

45. This 1953 RAF aerial photograph shows:

i) The effectiveness of the 1940 revetments and groynes at Craig-y-bwch; Point A;

ii) The location of the Corris Railway bridge; the damage caused by the river, and the revetments which were erected *after* the railway's closure, to control the river; area of Point B;

iii) Location of the culvert; Point C; and

iv) Point D, re-entry of the old course of the river to the main stream of the Dyfi, east of Dyfi Bridge.
Crown Copyright

46. The river damage which closed the line. To all intents and purposes, erosion progressed no further than this point. Even at this late hour, closure could have been averted speedily and surprisingly cheaply; there was no shortage of slate waste to fill the breach.   *H. C. Casserley*

47. Reverse view from No. 46 looking north, towards Ffridd Gate. A careful visual check of the alignment of the rails at both ends of the bridge will support the view of the older drivers who were critical of this aspect of the steel bridge. Those who had experience of crossing both bridges in their time were firmly of the opinion that the new bridge was not surveyed as well as it might have been, as drivers of 'up' trains, particularly, were inhibited from 'rushing' the 1 in 32 bank as they might have wished.   *H. C. Casserley*

36

48. An excellent view from the bridge, looking south, illustrating the river's determination to reach its old course, approximately in line with the distant hedgerow. Main line activity around the shed and station in the background could often result in flourishes of steam from several locomotives at a time; on this occasion, only the yard engine makes any notable contribution.
H. C. Casserley

49. This blurred view still manages to convey the awsome conditions which prevail when the Dyfi is in flood and suggests that in the past, drivers displayed considerable confidence in the fidelity of the bridge before taking a train across the open girders and into the flood waters beyond. Absence of the plank-way between the rails indicates this view may be dated *c.* 1928-1930.
Corris Railway Society Archives

50. The approach to Ffridd Woods, looking in the 'up' direction. Despite periodic dousing with weed-killer, generous rainfall ensured a prolific growth of grasses at certain points along the route. *H. C. Casserley*

51. Ffridd Woods, approaching Dolderwen; 'up' direction. *H. C. Casserley*

52. The curve beyond Abergarfan; again, looking 'up'. *H. C. Casserley*

53. Ffridd Woods curve, looking 'down' towards Ffridd Gate. Although the grass is plentiful, the rail alignment is obviously of a high order. The nearby Tal-y-llyn Railway had to wait several years before it could achieve this standard. The leat was for the nearby Ffridd mill at Glan-gwynedd. *H. C. Casserley*

54. No train had run through the station at Corris for over a month since closure, but the hand truck on the platform, the road trailer parked behind the station building and the smoke emerging from the chimney of the parcels office all indicate some vestige of life in the system, even though the trains had ceased. 23 September 1948.

R.K. Cope/Roger Carpenter

55. The end of the line; Machynlleth station after the closure. The guards' van had been moved alongside the old coaling stage, its brake screwed down hard and the door padlocked in order to contain the remaining Corris rolling-stock within a resticted area. The point at which the last of the buried rails had been removed from in front of the station is plain to see, as is the growing colony of Japanese knotweed. Finally, this view also illustrates the comparative levels of station building and track. Had sufficient finance been available when the station was rebuilt *c.* 1904, it is possible a wide platform could have been constucted here. Photographed on 13 September 1949.

R. K. Cope/Roger Carpenter

56. Corris rolling-stock awaiting its fate; an undated photograph *c.* 1949-50, from the era of road trailer operation (extreme left).
Boughey/courtesy John Keylock

57. The partially dismantled No. 4 *en route* to Leeds, complete with label tied to the back-sheet, rests in the lower yard at Machynlleth, 21 February 1952.
GBJ

58. The end of the line; the white gate marked the boundary between the railway and the tramway which served the quarries at Aberllefenni, although, in practice, both the railway's steel rails and the locomotives encroached for a few yards beyond the gate. The white 6½ mile post was still *in situ* when this photograph was taken on 13 September 1949. *R. K. Cope/Roger Carpenter*

59. The driver of a grey Ferguson tractor attends to the coupling between his motive power and 'train' as he set out to collect some newly-quarried rock for the slate mill at Aberllefenni, September 1970. *Roger Kidner*

60. Some of the final remains of the old line. The former carriage shed still continues as a coal store; the stable block, now occupied by the Corris Society, lies beyond on the right-hand side whilst, to the left, a most valuable stock of rails rests where the platform was located. An undated photograph but *c.* 1949.

NRM/Selwyn Pearce Higgins

61. A high flood encroaches on the Machynlleth Low Level site (station extreme left). Photographed from the rear of the former Ratgoed wharf, *c.*1953. *GBJ*

62. Pre-Second World War Maes-poeth, *c.* 1939, included for comparison with the contemporary view below.

Photomatic.

63. The new railway. Damp and dreary conditions fail to diminish the impact of recent progress at Maes-poeth. The well-ballasted track, the new signal-box, stacks of new hardwood sleepers, the ex-Trecŵn MoD guards' van and the dedicated ballast waggons on the upper level all pay silent tribute to the time, money and energy spent by volunteers; 31 March 2001.

GBJ

64. The approach to Corris in 1935.   *J. K. S. Clarke, courtesy Roger Kidner*

65. The approach to Corris, 30 March 2001. The former signal-cabin was set into the wall which has since been made good and does not, as yet, harbour any moss, lichen or ferns. The portakabin, the village's medical centre, occupies the location of the former passenger platform but the distinctive sloping roof of the old stable block-cum-museum is visible in both views.   *GBJ*

THE CORRIS RAILWAY SOCIETY

The Corris Railway Society was founded in 1966, with the twin aims of studying the history of the railway and district, and opening a museum dedicated to the line. Following an unsuccessful attempt to purchase Machynlleth station, the old stable block at Corris station became the home of the Corris Railway Museum, with the first section opening in 1970. The museum has been enlarged as repairs to the building made more of it useable, and is open during the holiday season and at other times by arrangement.

The first section of rail for a 'demonstration track' was re-laid in 1971, close to the museum. By the mid-1970s, the society felt confident that it could reopen part of the line to passengers, and so incorporated the Corris Railway Company Ltd in 1977, to take over the railway side of the society's operations, while the society was registered as an educational charity.

Planning permission was granted for a line from Corris to Maes-poeth, and following negotiations with the concerned authorities, broad agreement was reached for a further two miles, to the Forestry Commission picnic site at Tan-y-coed. However, a lack of co-operation from the planning authorities meant that there was a thirteen-year delay before outline planning permission was finally received in 1994. During that period the Light Railway Order for which the society had been aiming had been superseded by the more complicated Transport & Works Order, and further delay has been caused by the need to comply with the new requirements. At the time of writing (March 2001), good progress has been made on this front but it is still not possible to give a firm date for the recommencement of passenger services.

While the negotiations with the various authorities have been taking place, the railway has made great strides on the ground. The acquisition of Maes-poeth sheds in 1981 was a major boost to the project and in tandem with the refurbishment of the building has been the installation of machinery that largely restores the pre-1930 position, when the Corris was able to carry out all but the heaviest engineering work in-house.

Track of passenger-carrying standard has been reinstated from Maes-poeth to Corris, along with the fencing and drainage, which had all but vanished during the years of closure. The site of Corris station building is currently occupied by a portakabin, used as a medical centre, and the society has installed a new platform in the remaining space at the southern end of the site.

Three diesel locomotives have been acquired. No. 5, *Alan Meaden* (named after the society's founder) is a lightweight product of Motor Rail, works number 22258 of 1965, and originally used on the 2ft gauge system at Hindlow in Derbyshire. After re-gauging, it arrived on Corris metals in 1980, and has since proved invaluable in helping with the reconstruction of the track.

No. 6, Ruston Hornsby 518493 of 1966, was acquired from the 2ft 6ins gauge system at BICC, Prescot, Merseyside, in 1982. It has been extensively overhauled, including the fitting of a new cab and running boards, and came into service in 1996. It has been fitted with air-braking equipment to allow it to haul the initial passenger services.

No. 8 is a product of the Hunslet Engine Company and is on loan from the National Mining Museum; so far, its works number has not been identified. At the time of writing, it is being overhauled away from Corris but is expected to make its first run on Corris metals before the end of the year 2001. It is also being fitted with air-braking equipment to allow it to operate passenger services.

The railway has also launched a project to

construct a brand-new steam locomotive, based on the Kerr Stuart 'Tattoo' class to which No. 4 belongs. This is being built by Winson Engineering of Daventry, and has been allocated the number 7 in the Corris stock list. Supporters of the project have taken out covenants, guaranteeing a steady flow of income, and the locomotive is being constructed section by section as funds permit. At the end of 2000, frames, wheels, cylinders, motion, boiler, smoke-box, firebox and chimney were all substantially complete and it is anticipated that No. 7 will be ready to reintroduce steam haulage to the Dulas valley soon after the railway gets the green light to recommence passenger services.

A varied collection of rolling-stock has been assembled on the railway, some brought in from elsewhere and adapted for Corris use (usually involving re-gauging from either 2ft or 2ft 6ins), others built up using salvaged original Corris or quarry material. For the future passenger service, an ex-Royal Navy brake van has been converted to suit Corris requirements. This joins the first new passenger carriage on the railway for almost a century, No. 20 *Tiger*, constructed on a four-wheel manrider chassis with a wooden body based on the design of the original bogie vehicles, with two saloons and a centre vestibule. Currently, type approval is being sought for a new bogie carriage system, which will appear similar to the originals but be constructed to modern safety standards.

A recent innovation has been the creation of a rake of 'Heritage Waggons', with the railway's original waggon No. 7 (GW 31995) returned from the Tal-y-llyn and restored, joined by a similar metal-bodied waggon from Aberllefenni quarry and a replica slab waggon, a design unique to the Corris. A fourth waggon, a two-plank tie-rod open, is currently undergoing restoration. Together with the carriage and brake van, these give a good idea of how a mixed train on the line would have appeared in the 1920s.

The year 1996 marked the seventy-fifth anniversary of locomotive No. 4's arrival at Corris, and to mark the occasion, the society arranged with the Tal-y-llyn Railway for the loco to return to its original home for a fortnight in October. Accompanied by the original Corris brake van, the restored Corris mail waggon and an ex-Corris coal waggon, a red-liveried No. 4 made a number of runs from Maes-poeth up to Corris, and provided not only a memory of the old days on the line, but a taste of the future, as everyone involved looked forward to the day when steam-hauled passenger services will once again be a regular occurrence in the Dulas valley.

Richard S. Greenhough
on behalf of the Corris Railway Society
March 2001

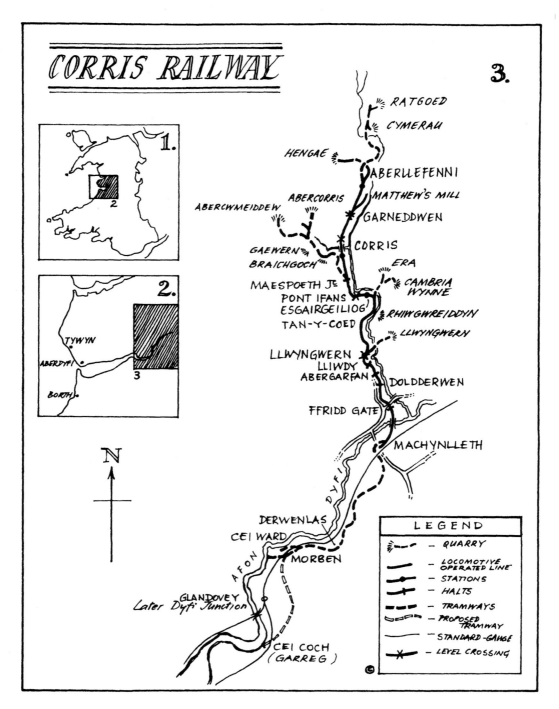

CORRIS RAILWAY

3.

RATGOED
CYMERAU
HENGAE
ABERLLEFENNI
ABERCORRIS
MATTHEW'S MILL
ABERCWMEIDDEW
GARNEDDWEN
CORRIS
GAEWERN
BRAICHGOCH
ERA
CAMBRIA
WYNNE
MAESPOETH Jⁿ
PONT IFANS
ESGAIRGEILIOG
TAN-Y-COED
RHIWGWREIDDYN
LLWYNGWERN
LLWYNGWERN
LLIWDY
ABERGARFAN
DOLDDERWEN
FFRIDD GATE
MACHYNLLETH
DYFI
DERWENLAS
CEI WARD
MORBEN
AFON
GLANDOVEY
Later Dyfi Junction
CEI COCH
(GARREG)

N

LEGEND

‑ ‑ ‑	QUARRY
━━━	LOCOMOTIVE OPERATED LINE
●━●	STATIONS
┼━┼	HALTS
▬ ▬ ▬	TRAMWAYS
▬ ▬	PROPOSED TRAMWAY
━━━	STANDARD-GAUGE
✳	LEVEL CROSSING

1.

2.
TYWYN
ABERDYFI
BORTH
3

48